EMMANUEL JOSEPH

Blueprints and Bytes, Human Strategies from Valley Visionaries and Property Moguls

Copyright © 2025 by Emmanuel Joseph

All rights reserved. No part of this publication may be reproduced, stored or transmitted in any form or by any means, electronic, mechanical, photocopying, recording, scanning, or otherwise without written permission from the publisher. It is illegal to copy this book, post it to a website, or distribute it by any other means without permission.

First edition

This book was professionally typeset on Reedsy.
Find out more at reedsy.com

Contents

1	Chapter 1: The Dawn of Innovation	1
2	Chapter 2: Building the Foundation	3
3	Chapter 3: The Power of Adaptability	5
4	Chapter 4: Cultivating Relationships	7
5	Chapter 5: Embracing Technology	9
6	Chapter 6: Visionary Leadership	11
7	Chapter 7: Risk Management	13
8	Chapter 8: Financial Acumen	15
9	Chapter 9: Innovation and Creativity	17
10	Chapter 10: Social Responsibility	20
11	Chapter 11: Future Trends	22
12	Chapter 12: Legacy and Impact	24

1

Chapter 1: The Dawn of Innovation

Silicon Valley's rise as the epicenter of technological advancement didn't happen overnight. It started with the passion and persistence of pioneers like Steve Jobs, Bill Gates, and many others. These visionaries saw potential in personal computing and digital communication long before it was mainstream. Their journey was marked by constant experimentation, numerous failures, and relentless pursuit of their dreams. They taught the world that innovation isn't just about having a great idea; it's about the determination to bring that idea to life, despite the challenges.

Their stories are a testament to the power of vision. Jobs, for instance, envisioned a world where technology was accessible and intuitive for everyone. This vision drove Apple's early innovations and continues to influence its products today. Gates, on the other hand, saw the potential of software to transform businesses and everyday life. His work at Microsoft set the standard for personal and business computing. These early innovators didn't just create products; they created industries and set the stage for the digital revolution.

The foundations they laid were not only technological but also philosophical. They challenged traditional business models and introduced new ways of thinking about entrepreneurship and innovation. They showed that success often comes from taking risks and being willing to challenge the status quo. This mindset has become a cornerstone of Silicon Valley's culture, fostering an environment where creativity and innovation thrive.

Their influence extends beyond technology. The principles they championed—such as the importance of a clear vision, the willingness to take risks, and the value of perseverance—are relevant across all industries. For real estate moguls, these principles can be applied to property development and management, emphasizing the importance of forward-thinking strategies and the courage to pursue ambitious projects.

In essence, the dawn of innovation in Silicon Valley was not just about technological breakthroughs. It was about a new way of thinking and doing business that has since permeated various industries, including real estate. By learning from these early pioneers, entrepreneurs in all fields can cultivate the mindset and strategies needed to achieve lasting success.

2

Chapter 2: Building the Foundation

A strong foundation is crucial for any successful venture, whether in technology or real estate. For property moguls like Donald Bren and Stephen Ross, understanding the market, thorough planning, and strategic location were key to their success. They didn't just build properties; they created thriving communities that met the needs of their residents and businesses.

Market research is the first step in building a solid foundation. Successful developers understand the importance of analyzing market trends, demographics, and economic factors. This knowledge allows them to identify opportunities and make informed decisions about where and what to build. Bren's success with the Irvine Company, for example, is a result of his deep understanding of the Southern California market and his ability to anticipate future growth.

Strategic planning is another critical component. Real estate development involves numerous moving parts, from financing and construction to marketing and sales. Effective planning ensures that all these elements come together seamlessly. Ross's development of Hudson Yards in New York City is a prime example of meticulous planning and coordination. The project transformed a previously underutilized area into a vibrant, mixed-use community.

Financial management is also essential. Real estate ventures require significant capital investments, and managing these resources effectively can make or break a project. Successful developers employ sound financial strategies to ensure their projects are viable and profitable. This includes securing financing, budgeting, and managing costs throughout the development process.

Location is a key factor in real estate success. The adage "location, location, location" holds true, as the right location can significantly impact a property's value and appeal. Developers like Bren and Ross have a keen eye for identifying prime locations that offer growth potential and align with market demand. Their ability to choose the right sites has been instrumental in their success.

In conclusion, building a strong foundation is essential for success in both technology and real estate. By understanding the market, planning strategically, managing finances effectively, and choosing the right locations, entrepreneurs can set the stage for long-term success and growth.

3

Chapter 3: The Power of Adaptability

Adaptability is a crucial trait for success in any industry, but it is especially important in the fast-paced worlds of technology and real estate. The ability to pivot and respond to changing circumstances can mean the difference between success and failure. Silicon Valley entrepreneurs like Mark Zuckerberg and Elon Musk have demonstrated this time and again, showing that flexibility and openness to change are key to staying relevant and competitive.

In technology, the pace of change is rapid, and those who can adapt quickly are the ones who thrive. Zuckerberg's journey with Facebook is a prime example. What started as a social networking site for college students quickly evolved into a global platform with diverse offerings, from advertising to virtual reality. Zuckerberg's willingness to pivot and adapt to new opportunities has been a major factor in Facebook's enduring success.

Similarly, Musk's ventures, from Tesla to SpaceX, highlight the importance of adaptability. When faced with challenges, Musk has shown a remarkable ability to change course and find innovative solutions. Whether it's rethinking electric vehicle production or developing reusable rockets, his flexibility has enabled him to push the boundaries of what's possible and achieve groundbreaking success.

In real estate, adaptability is equally important. Market conditions, economic shifts, and evolving consumer preferences can all impact the success of a development. Developers who can adapt to these changes are better positioned to succeed. For example, during economic downturns, some developers have shifted their focus from luxury properties to more affordable housing to meet changing demand.

Adaptability also means being open to new ideas and technologies. Real estate developers who embrace advancements like smart home technology, green building practices, and virtual property tours can stay ahead of the curve and attract modern buyers. Integrating these innovations into their projects allows them to offer added value and differentiate themselves in a competitive market.

In both tech and real estate, adaptability is a critical factor for long-term success. By staying flexible, embracing change, and being open to new opportunities, entrepreneurs can navigate challenges and continue to grow and innovate. This chapter underscores the importance of adaptability and provides strategies for cultivating this essential trait.

4

Chapter 4: Cultivating Relationships

Building strong relationships is a cornerstone of success in both technology and real estate. No one achieves greatness alone, and the ability to forge meaningful connections can significantly impact an entrepreneur's journey. Tech leaders and property moguls alike emphasize the importance of collaboration, trust, and effective communication in their dealings with partners, clients, and communities.

In Silicon Valley, the power of networks is well understood. Tech entrepreneurs often rely on their connections for funding, mentorship, and support. Venture capitalists, fellow entrepreneurs, and industry experts form a web of relationships that can open doors and provide valuable insights. This collaborative environment fosters innovation and helps startups navigate the challenges of growth and scaling.

Property developers, too, recognize the value of strong relationships. Trust and reliability are critical when working with contractors, investors, and clients. Developers who cultivate a reputation for integrity and dependability are more likely to attract and retain valuable partners. This trust extends to the communities they serve, where transparent communication and community engagement can build goodwill and support for their projects.

Effective communication is key to building and maintaining relationships. In both tech and real estate, clear and open lines of communication can prevent misunderstandings, resolve conflicts, and ensure that all parties are aligned with the project's goals. Successful leaders prioritize communication, actively listening to feedback, and addressing concerns promptly.

Collaboration is another essential aspect. In technology, cross-functional teams bring together diverse expertise to develop innovative solutions. Real estate projects often involve a wide range of professionals, from architects and engineers to marketers and sales teams. Fostering a collaborative environment where everyone works towards a common goal can lead to more successful and efficient outcomes.

Building strong relationships also involves giving back and supporting others. Mentorship and knowledge sharing are common in both industries, with experienced leaders guiding and supporting the next generation of entrepreneurs. This culture of support helps create a thriving ecosystem where everyone benefits from shared success.

In summary, cultivating relationships is a vital strategy for achieving success in both technology and real estate. By building trust, prioritizing communication, fostering collaboration, and supporting others, entrepreneurs can create a network of meaningful connections that drive growth and innovation.

5

Chapter 5: Embracing Technology

Technology is a transformative force, reshaping industries and creating new opportunities. In the real estate sector, embracing technology can revolutionize how properties are marketed, managed, and sold. From virtual tours and AI-powered property management systems to blockchain and smart home technology, the integration of tech innovations is enhancing the real estate experience for both developers and buyers.

Virtual tours have become a game-changer in property marketing. They allow potential buyers to explore properties from the comfort of their homes, providing an immersive experience that goes beyond traditional photos and videos. This technology not only saves time but also broadens the reach of property listings, attracting buyers from different regions and even countries. Developers who leverage virtual tours can showcase their properties more effectively and stand out in a competitive market.

AI-powered property management systems are transforming the way properties are maintained and operated. These systems use data analytics and machine learning to optimize property performance, predict maintenance needs, and streamline operations. For example, AI can monitor energy usage, detect potential issues before they become problems, and automate routine tasks, such as scheduling maintenance. This not only improves efficiency but also enhances the overall experience for tenants and property owners.

Blockchain technology is making waves in real estate transactions. By providing a secure and transparent way to record and verify transactions, blockchain can streamline the buying and selling process, reduce fraud, and lower transaction costs. Smart contracts, powered by blockchain, can automate and enforce agreements, ensuring that all parties meet their obligations. This technology has the potential to revolutionize real estate transactions, making them faster, more secure, and more efficient.

Smart home technology is another innovation that is gaining traction in the real estate market. From smart thermostats and lighting systems to security thermostats and lighting systems to security cameras and home automation, smart home technology is enhancing the comfort, convenience, and security of modern living spaces. Developers who incorporate these features into their properties can offer added value and attract tech-savvy buyers who are looking for the latest in home innovation.

Integrating technology into real estate development is not without its challenges. Developers must stay informed about the latest advancements and be willing to invest in new systems and training. Additionally, the implementation of technology must be carefully planned to ensure it enhances rather than disrupts the overall living experience. However, the potential benefits of embracing technology far outweigh the challenges, offering new ways to improve efficiency, reduce costs, and enhance the appeal of properties.

In conclusion, technology is a powerful tool that can revolutionize the real estate industry. By embracing innovations like virtual tours, AI-powered property management, blockchain, and smart home technology, developers can stay ahead of the curve and offer enhanced value to their clients. This chapter highlights the importance of staying informed and open to new opportunities, ensuring long-term success in a rapidly evolving market.

6

Chapter 6: Visionary Leadership

Visionary leadership is a defining characteristic of successful entrepreneurs in both technology and real estate. Great leaders are not only adept at making strategic decisions but also at inspiring and motivating their teams to achieve common goals. In Silicon Valley, visionary leaders like Steve Jobs, Elon Musk, and Jeff Bezos have driven their companies to remarkable heights through their unique leadership styles and unwavering commitment to their visions.

In the tech world, visionary leadership often involves a willingness to challenge the status quo and push the boundaries of what is possible. Steve Jobs, for example, was known for his relentless pursuit of excellence and his ability to inspire his team to create groundbreaking products. His leadership style was characterized by a clear vision, attention to detail, and an uncompromising dedication to quality. This approach not only led to the creation of iconic products but also fostered a culture of innovation and creativity within Apple.

Elon Musk's leadership at Tesla and SpaceX is another example of visionary leadership. Musk's audacious goals, such as colonizing Mars and accelerating the transition to sustainable energy, have captivated the public's imagination and rallied his teams around a shared mission. His ability to articulate a compelling vision and drive his teams to overcome seemingly insurmountable challenges has been a key factor in his success.

In real estate, visionary leadership involves not only strategic planning and execution but also a deep understanding of the market and a commitment to creating value for stakeholders. Developers like Stephen Ross have demonstrated the importance of visionary leadership in transforming urban spaces and creating vibrant communities. Ross's development of Hudson Yards, for example, required a bold vision and the ability to navigate complex regulatory and financial landscapes. His leadership ensured that the project not only met market demands but also enhanced the overall quality of life for residents and visitors.

Effective leadership in both industries also involves the ability to inspire and motivate teams. Great leaders understand that their success depends on the efforts of their teams and prioritize creating a positive and supportive work environment. This includes fostering open communication, recognizing and rewarding contributions, and providing opportunities for growth and development. By empowering their teams and creating a culture of collaboration and innovation, visionary leaders can drive their organizations to achieve remarkable success.

In summary, visionary leadership is a critical factor in the success of entrepreneurs in both technology and real estate. By articulating a clear vision, challenging the status quo, and inspiring and motivating their teams, great leaders can drive innovation and achieve long-term success. This chapter explores the qualities that define visionary leaders and provides insights into how to cultivate effective leadership in any industry.

7

Chapter 7: Risk Management

Risk management is an essential aspect of entrepreneurship, particularly in the dynamic fields of technology and real estate. Every business venture involves some level of risk, and the ability to identify, assess, and mitigate these risks can mean the difference between success and failure. Successful entrepreneurs understand that while risk cannot be eliminated, it can be managed strategically to minimize negative impacts and capitalize on opportunities.

In technology, the pace of innovation and the competitive nature of the industry create unique risks. Tech entrepreneurs must navigate the uncertainties of developing new products, securing funding, and staying ahead of competitors. Successful leaders like Mark Zuckerberg and Jeff Bezos have demonstrated the importance of calculated risk-taking. By carefully assessing potential risks and making informed decisions, they have been able to seize opportunities and drive their companies to success.

Real estate development also involves significant risks, from fluctuating market conditions to regulatory challenges and construction delays. Developers must have a keen understanding of these risks and develop strategies to mitigate them. This includes conducting thorough market research, securing reliable financing, and establishing contingency plans for potential setbacks. Successful developers like Donald Bren have shown that effective risk management is critical to the success of large-scale projects.

One key aspect of risk management is diversification. In both technology and real estate, diversifying investments and projects can help spread risk and reduce exposure to potential losses. Tech companies often invest in a range of products and services to hedge against market volatility. Similarly, real estate developers may pursue a mix of residential, commercial, and mixed-use projects to balance their portfolios and ensure steady revenue streams.

Another important strategy is contingency planning. Entrepreneurs who anticipate potential risks and develop contingency plans are better prepared to respond to unexpected challenges. This includes having backup plans for financing, alternative suppliers, and strategies for addressing market downturns. By planning for the unexpected, entrepreneurs can navigate uncertainties with confidence and resilience.

Risk management also involves staying informed and adaptable. The ability to monitor market trends, regulatory changes, and emerging opportunities is crucial for making informed decisions. Entrepreneurs who stay abreast of industry developments and remain flexible in their approach can adjust their strategies as needed to mitigate risks and capitalize on new opportunities.

In conclusion, risk management is a vital component of successful entrepreneurship in both technology and real estate. By identifying, assessing, and mitigating risks, entrepreneurs can navigate uncertainties and achieve long-term success. This chapter provides insights into effective risk management strategies and highlights the importance of staying informed, adaptable, and prepared for the unexpected.

8

Chapter 8: Financial Acumen

Financial acumen is a critical skill for entrepreneurs in both technology and real estate. Mastering the financial aspects of a business, from securing funding to managing budgets and ensuring profitability, is essential for building a successful and sustainable venture. Tech giants and property developers alike have demonstrated the importance of sound financial planning and strategic investment in their journeys to success.

In the technology sector, securing funding is often one of the first challenges entrepreneurs face. Startups typically rely on venture capital, angel investors, or crowdfunding to raise the necessary capital for development and growth. Successful tech leaders understand the importance of crafting compelling pitches and demonstrating the potential for high returns to attract investors. Once funding is secured, effective financial management is crucial to ensure that resources are allocated efficiently and that the company remains on track to achieve its goals.

Budgeting and cost management are also essential components of financial acumen. Tech companies must carefully manage their expenses, from research and development to marketing and operations, to ensure they stay within budget and maximize their resources. This requires a deep understanding of the company's financial health and the ability to make strategic decisions that balance short-term needs with long-term growth.

In real estate, financial acumen involves understanding the intricacies of property financing, investment analysis, and revenue management. Developers must secure funding for their projects, whether through traditional bank loans, private equity, or other financing mechanisms. Successful developers like Stephen Ross have demonstrated the importance of structuring deals that provide sufficient capital while minimizing risk. This involves negotiating favorable terms, understanding market conditions, and assessing the financial viability of each project.

Investment analysis is another critical skill for real estate entrepreneurs. This involves evaluating potential projects based on factors such as location, market demand, and projected returns. By conducting thorough due diligence and analyzing financial metrics, developers can make informed decisions that maximize profitability. Additionally, effective revenue management ensures that properties generate consistent income and maintain their value over time.

Profitability is the ultimate goal for any business, and achieving it requires a combination of financial discipline, strategic investment, and cost management. Entrepreneurs in both technology and real estate must continuously monitor their financial performance, identify areas for improvement, and make adjustments as needed. This proactive approach to financial management helps ensure long-term sustainability and growth.

In summary, financial acumen is a vital skill for entrepreneurs in both technology and real estate. By securing funding, managing budgets, analyzing investments, and ensuring profitability, entrepreneurs can build financially robust businesses that thrive in any economic climate. This chapter provides practical insights into mastering the financial aspects of entrepreneurship and highlights the importance of strategic financial planning and management.

9

Chapter 9: Innovation and Creativity

Innovation and creativity are the lifeblood of progress, driving technological advancements and transforming urban landscapes. In both technology and real estate, the ability to think creatively and push the boundaries of what is possible is essential for staying competitive and achieving long-term success. Silicon Valley's culture of relentless innovation has produced some of the world's most groundbreaking technologies, while visionary developers have reimagined urban spaces to meet the needs of modern society.

In the tech industry, innovation is a constant pursuit. Companies like Apple, Google, and Amazon have built their success on a foundation of continuous innovation, constantly developing new products and services that revolutionize the way we live and work. This culture of innovation is driven by a willingness to experiment, take risks, and embrace failure as a learning opportunity. By fostering an environment where creativity is encouraged and rewarded, these companies have been able to stay at the forefront of technological advancements.

Real estate developers also rely on innovation to create unique and valuable properties. Visionary developers like Frank Gehry and Zaha Hadid have pushed the boundaries of architectural design, creating iconic structures that redefine urban landscapes. Their innovative approaches to design and construction have not only set new standards for aesthetics and functionality but have also created spaces that enhance the quality of life for residents and visitors. By embracing creativity and challenging conventional norms, these developers have made lasting contributions to the field of real estate.

Innovation in real estate extends beyond architecture to include sustainable practices and smart technologies. Green building techniques, such as energy-efficient materials, renewable energy sources, and sustainable water management, are becoming increasingly important in urban development. By incorporating these practices, developers can create environmentally friendly buildings that reduce carbon footprints and promote sustainability. This commitment to innovation not only benefits the environment but also enhances the market appeal of properties.

Smart technologies are also transforming the real estate landscape. From smart home devices that offer convenience and security to intelligent building management systems that optimize energy use and maintenance, technology is enhancing the functionality and efficiency of properties. Developers who integrate these technologies into their projects can offer residents a modern, connected living experience that meets the demands of today's tech-savvy consumers.

Fostering an innovative mindset requires a willingness to take risks and explore new ideas. Entrepreneurs in both technology and real estate must be open to experimentation and unafraid of failure. Successful innovators understand that not every idea will succeed, but each failure provides valuable lessons that can lead to future success. By creating an environment where creativity is encouraged and failure is viewed as a learning opportunity, businesses can cultivate a culture of innovation.

Collaboration is another key driver of innovation. Cross-functional teams, diverse perspectives, and partnerships with external organizations can spark new ideas and solutions. In technology, collaboration between engineers, designers, and marketers often leads to groundbreaking products. In real estate, partnerships with architects, urban planners, and technology providers can result in innovative projects that push the boundaries of what's possible. By fostering a collaborative environment, entrepreneurs can tap into a wealth of creativity and drive innovation.

CHAPTER 9: INNOVATION AND CREATIVITY

In conclusion, innovation and creativity are essential for success in both technology and real estate. By embracing new ideas, taking risks, and fostering a culture of collaboration, entrepreneurs can drive progress and create transformative solutions. This chapter celebrates the power of innovation and provides strategies for cultivating an innovative mindset, ensuring long-term success in a rapidly evolving landscape.

10

Chapter 10: Social Responsibility

With great success comes great responsibility. Entrepreneurs in both technology and real estate have a profound impact on society and the environment, and it is essential for them to incorporate social responsibility into their business practices. By prioritizing ethical considerations, sustainability, and community engagement, businesses can create positive change while achieving their goals.

In the technology sector, social responsibility often involves addressing issues such as data privacy, digital inclusion, and environmental impact. Tech companies must ensure that their products and services protect user privacy and data security. This includes implementing robust security measures, transparent data practices, and user-friendly privacy controls. Additionally, promoting digital inclusion by providing access to technology for underserved communities can help bridge the digital divide and create opportunities for economic growth.

Environmental sustainability is another critical aspect of social responsibility in technology. Companies can reduce their carbon footprint by adopting energy-efficient practices, utilizing renewable energy sources, and minimizing electronic waste. By integrating sustainability into their operations, tech companies can contribute to global efforts to combat climate change and promote environmental stewardship.

In real estate, social responsibility involves sustainable development, com-

CHAPTER 10: SOCIAL RESPONSIBILITY

munity engagement, and equitable housing practices. Developers can adopt green building techniques, such as using eco-friendly materials, implementing energy-efficient designs, and promoting sustainable transportation options. These practices not only benefit the environment but also enhance the quality of life for residents and contribute to the long-term viability of properties.

Community engagement is also vital for socially responsible real estate development. Developers who actively involve local communities in the planning and decision-making processes can build trust and foster positive relationships. This includes seeking input from residents, addressing community concerns, and ensuring that projects benefit the local area. By prioritizing community engagement, developers can create projects that are not only profitable but also enhance the social fabric of the communities they serve.

Equitable housing practices are essential for addressing housing affordability and accessibility issues. Developers can contribute to social equity by incorporating affordable housing units into their projects, supporting inclusive zoning policies, and partnering with non-profit organizations to provide housing for underserved populations. By promoting equitable housing, developers can help create diverse, inclusive communities that offer opportunities for all residents.

In summary, social responsibility is a critical component of successful entrepreneurship in both technology and real estate. By prioritizing ethical considerations, sustainability, and community engagement, businesses can create positive change while achieving their goals. This chapter highlights the importance of social responsibility and provides strategies for integrating it into business practices, ensuring long-term success and positive impact.

11

Chapter 11: Future Trends

Staying ahead of emerging trends is crucial for long-term success in both technology and real estate. The future is full of possibilities, and entrepreneurs who anticipate and embrace these trends can position themselves at the forefront of their industries. This chapter explores some of the key trends shaping the future of technology and real estate, offering insights into how to navigate and capitalize on these changes.

One significant trend in technology is the continued advancement of artificial intelligence (AI) and machine learning. These technologies are transforming various industries, from healthcare and finance to retail and entertainment. In real estate, AI-powered tools are revolutionizing property management, marketing, and investment analysis. By leveraging AI, developers can enhance efficiency, improve decision-making, and offer personalized experiences to clients.

The rise of smart cities is another trend with far-reaching implications for both technology and real estate. Smart cities integrate advanced technologies, such as IoT (Internet of Things), data analytics, and renewable energy, to create more efficient, sustainable, and livable urban environments. Developers who embrace smart city principles can create innovative projects that address the needs of modern urban dwellers, from smart homes and connected infrastructure to sustainable transportation and green spaces.

Sustainability is an ongoing trend that will continue to shape the future of both industries. As environmental concerns grow, there is increasing demand for sustainable practices and products. In technology, this includes developing energy-efficient devices, reducing electronic waste, and adopting circular economy principles. In real estate, sustainable building practices, renewable energy integration, and green certifications are becoming standard requirements. By prioritizing sustainability, entrepreneurs can meet market demand and contribute to global efforts to combat climate change.

The concept of co-living and co-working spaces is gaining traction as urbanization and changing work patterns drive demand for flexible, community-oriented living and working arrangements. Co-living spaces offer shared amenities and a sense of community, appealing to young professionals and urban residents. Co-working spaces provide flexible work environments that cater to freelancers, remote workers, and small businesses. Developers who incorporate these concepts into their projects can tap into a growing market and meet the evolving needs of residents and workers.

Lastly, the integration of virtual and augmented reality (VR/AR) is transforming the way properties are marketed and experienced. Virtual tours, immersive property walkthroughs, and augmented reality design tools offer new ways to engage potential buyers and tenants. By adopting VR/AR technologies, developers can enhance the property viewing experience and differentiate themselves in a competitive market.

In conclusion, staying ahead of future trends is essential for long-term success in technology and real estate. By anticipating and embracing advancements in AI, smart cities, sustainability, co-living, and VR/AR, entrepreneurs can position themselves at the forefront of their industries and continue to drive innovation. This chapter provides insights into key trends shaping the future and offers strategies for navigating and capitalizing on these changes.

12

Chapter 12: Legacy and Impact

Ultimately, the legacy we leave behind reflects the impact we've made on the world. Successful entrepreneurs in both technology and real estate understand that their work has the potential to create lasting change and improve the lives of countless individuals. This chapter examines the legacies of some of the most influential figures in these industries, highlighting the lessons we can learn from their journeys and the importance of making a positive impact.

In the technology sector, leaders like Steve Jobs, Bill Gates, and Elon Musk have left indelible marks on the world. Their contributions extend beyond the products and services they created; they have inspired generations of innovators and transformed entire industries. Jobs' emphasis on design and user experience revolutionized personal computing and consumer electronics. Gates' vision of a computer in every home and office paved the way for the digital age. Musk's ambitious goals for sustainable energy and space exploration continue to push the boundaries of what's possible.

In real estate, developers like Donald Bren and Stephen Ross have shaped urban landscapes and created communities that enhance the quality of life for residents. Bren's development of master-planned communities in Southern California has set new standards for residential living, combining thoughtful design, sustainability, and community amenities. Ross's transformative projects, such as Hudson Yards, demonstrate the potential of urban

CHAPTER 12: LEGACY AND IMPACT

development to revitalize neighborhoods and create vibrant, mixed-use environments. Their legacies are not just about the physical structures they built, but also about the communities they created and the positive impact they had on the lives of countless individuals. By prioritizing quality, sustainability, and community engagement, these developers have set a high standard for the industry and left a lasting legacy that will inspire future generations of real estate professionals.

Creating a lasting legacy requires a commitment to making a positive impact. This involves not only achieving personal success but also using one's influence and resources to contribute to the greater good. Entrepreneurs who prioritize social responsibility, environmental sustainability, and community well-being can create a legacy that extends beyond their immediate accomplishments and benefits society as a whole.

Philanthropy is one way that successful entrepreneurs can give back and create a lasting impact. Many tech leaders and real estate developers have established foundations and charitable organizations to support causes they care about. For example, Bill Gates and his wife Melinda founded the Bill & Melinda Gates Foundation, which focuses on global health, education, and poverty alleviation. Similarly, many real estate developers support affordable housing initiatives, community development projects, and environmental conservation efforts.

Mentorship is another powerful way to create a lasting legacy. By sharing their knowledge and experience with the next generation of entrepreneurs, successful leaders can inspire and guide future innovators. This creates a ripple effect, as those who are mentored go on to mentor others, creating a culture of support and continuous learning. This transfer of knowledge and values ensures that the principles of innovation, integrity, and social responsibility continue to thrive.

Ultimately, the legacy we leave behind is a reflection of the choices we make and the values we uphold. By striving to create positive change, prioritize social responsibility, and inspire others, entrepreneurs can leave a lasting impact that extends beyond their immediate achievements. This chapter encourages readers to think about the legacy they want to create and provides insights into how they can make a meaningful difference in their industries and communities.

Blueprints and Bytes: Human Strategies from Valley Visionaries and Property Moguls

In "Blueprints and Bytes," we dive into the intertwined worlds of technology and real estate to uncover the strategies that have propelled Silicon Valley's tech giants and property moguls to unprecedented success. This book is a rich tapestry of stories and lessons from visionaries like Steve Jobs and Elon Musk, to real estate titans like Donald Bren and Stephen Ross.

From the early days of innovation in Silicon Valley to the meticulous planning and market insights of property development, this book explores how adaptability, strong relationships, and visionary leadership have shaped industries and created lasting legacies. With chapters dedicated to financial acumen, the power of technology, and the importance of social responsibility, readers will gain a comprehensive understanding of what it takes to succeed in these dynamic fields.

Each chapter delves into the principles and practices that have defined the careers of these influential figures, offering insights into risk management, innovation, and the trends shaping the future. "Blueprints and Bytes" is not just a collection of strategies—it's a celebration of the spirit of creativity and the relentless pursuit of excellence that drives progress.

Whether you're an aspiring entrepreneur, a seasoned professional, or simply curious about the forces shaping our world, this book provides valuable lessons and inspiration. Discover how to build a strong foundation, embrace change, and create a lasting impact in your industry. "Blueprints and Bytes" is your guide to navigating the complexities of technology and real estate, and achieving success in the modern landscape.

www.ingramcontent.com/pod-product-compliance
Lightning Source LLC
LaVergne TN
LVHW020741090526
838202LV00057BA/6169